SOUTH TAHOE MIDDLE SCHOOL
P. O. Box 14426
So. Lake Tahoe, CA 95702

Factual Adviser
Dr. Jane Rendall
Lecturer in Modern History
University of York

Series and Book Editor: Nicole Lagneau
Teacher Panel: Maggie Howell, Brian Green, Cathy Loxton
Designer: Ewing Paddock
Production: Rosemary Bishop
Picture Research: Diana Morris

A MACDONALD BOOK

Printed and bound by Henri Proost
Turnhout, Belgium

Library of Congress Cataloging-in-Publication Data
Sproule, Anna.
    New ideas in industry.
    (Women history makers)
    Bibliography: p.
    Includes index.
    Summary: Examines the role of women in the industrial growth of the United States, France, and Great Britain through the lives of Catharine Greene, Nicole-Barbe Clicquot-Ponsardin, and Mary Quant.
    1. Women in business—United States—History—Case studies—Juvenile literature. 2. Women in business—France—History—Case studies—Juvenile literature. 3. Women in business—Great Britain—Case studies—Juvenile literature. 4. Greene, Catharine Littlefield—Juvenile literature.
5. Clicquot-Ponsardin, Nicole-Barbe, 1777–1866—Juvenile literature.
6. Quant, Mary—Juvenile literature. [1. Greene, Catharine Littlefield.
2. Clicquot-Ponsardin, Nicole-Barbe, 1777–1866. 3. Quant, Mary,
4. Women in business]
I. Title. II. Series.
HD6053.S67 1988   331.4′09   [920]   88–8566
ISBN 0–531–19502–3

Acknowledgements
We would like to thank Mary Quant for permission to quote from her autobiography, *Quant by Quant*. Also to Veuve Clicquot Ponsardin for permission to quote from *Madame Clicquot: Her Peaceful Conquest of Russia*, by Comte Bertrand de Vögué. To Patrick Forbes for permission to quote from *Champagne: the Wine, the Land, and the People*, Gollancz, 1967. To Barbara Bernard, for permission to quote from *Fashion in the '60s*, courtesy of Academy Editions, London.

We have made every effort to trace the owners of copyright material and acknowledge the source of quotes from the following:
The World of Eli Whitney, Jeannette Mirsky and Allan Nevins, Macmillan, N.Y., 1952.
The Fifties, Allen and Unwin, 1965.
The Young Pretenders, Professor J.B. Mays, Michael Joseph, 1965.
The Young Meteors by Jonathan Aitken, Secker & Warburg, 1967.
The Daily Mirror for the caption on Jean Shrimpton on page 37.
Caty: A Biography of Catharine Littlefield Greene, John and Janet Stegeman, first published by Rhode Island Bicentennial Foundation, 1977; 1985 edition published by the University of Georgia Press.
The Slave Community, by John W. Blassingame, OUP/NY, 1972.
The Industrial Revolution, Fontana Economic History of Europe, ed. C.M. Cipolla, 1973.

Illustrations:
Paul Cooper, pages 17, 25, 27

Photographs
Aldus Archive: 12, 26.
Barnaby's Picture Library: 33c, 36.
BBC Hulton Picture Library: 15t, 20 (Bettmann Archive), 34.
Camera Press; 9b, 32, 35c, 38.
Mary Evans Picture Library: 14, 30.
Format: 5 (Maggie Murray).
Holt Studios: 10b.
Peter Newark's Western Americana: 16, 17.
Photosource: 37r, 37l, 39t, 39b, 41, 43.
Mary Quant; cover r, 40.
Rex: 6-7, 33r, 35b.
Roger-Viollet: 23t, 24, 25.
Ann Ronan Picture Library: back cover, 10t, 13, 15b, 21, 23b, 27, 29.
Slater Mill Historic Site, R.I.; 11.
Telfair Academy of Arts and Sciences, Savannah: 8, 18.
University of Georgia Press: cover bl, 19.
Veuve Clicquot-Ponsardin: cover tl, 9t, 28, 31

Cover Captions:
Front top left: Veuve Clicquot-Ponsardin (1777–1866),
(see page 31).
Right: Mary Quant (b. 1934), (see page 41).
Bottom left: Catharine Greene (1755–1814) and Eli
Whitney (see pages 18–19).
Back cover: Slavery in the USA (see pages 14–15)

NEW IDEAS IN INDUSTRY

Anna Sproule

Hampstead Press New York 1988

About this book

Half the people in the world are women. But women seldom appear in books on history. One reason for this is that, until recently, historians have mostly written about public events; in the past, many people thought that women should not take part in these. But, all the same, some women managed to leave their mark on the public world around them.

In the past, many historians have shared the traditional view that a woman's real place was at home, serving her family. If they found proof against this view they often ignored it. If they found she influenced the world of public life from within her home setting, they often summed up achievements in a couple of sentences — or a footnote in small print. The books in this series aim to put the women history-makers back where they belong: in the world they helped change, and in the way that we remember that world.

The three women you will read about here all lived in periods of social and political change, in different countries. Catharine Greene lived through the American Revolution of the late 18th century. Nicole-Barbe Clicquot lived through the French Revolution, and the reign of Napoleon that followed it in the early 19th century. Designer Mary Quant helped lead the social revolution in Britain after World War II that gave young people their own special culture

How to use this book
When studying the past, historians try to go back to what the people of the past actually wrote and said. In the sections of this book marked "**Witness**," you can read some of the things said by people who were living at the time of Catharine Greene and Nicole-Barbe Clicquot, and who are living in Mary Quant's time today. You can also read comments from the women themselves. Keep a look out for these.

Women in industry, 1960: British designer Mary Quant watches as her designs are turned into clothes in a London workshop. Many industries in which women have become successful have strong links with domestic activities like dressmaking or cooking. In the 1980s, women are beginning to break into other industries.

Contents

Women and history

Every adult in the world who works takes part in making or doing things for themselves and others. They are all occupied in creating wealth for their families and their communities. This doesn't mean they're making themselves rich (though they would certainly like to). It means that they are producing the things that they need to live: food, shelter, clothing. Some farmers do it directly, by growing their own food. Industrial workers earn money that they convert into food and other necessities. They all take part in economic production.

Farming is one method of economic production. Industry is another. Today, we think of industry as meaning factories, production lines, crowds of machine and office workers. It is a much newer method than farming. It dates back no further than the 18th century, when the power of steam and water was first used to drive machines. Until then, goods were made by hand at home. But they could be made much more quickly by the new machines. Britain was the first country to go through this major industrial and social change, called the "Industrial Revolution."

It was during Catharine Greene's time that the US set up its first factories. Starting with the first cotton-spinning factory built in 1789, they were mainly in New England. Life was still geared to farming in the area where Catharine herself lived. But she helped invent one of the most important machines of all: the cotton gin.

Nicole-Barbe Clicquot lived in France during the 18th and 19th centuries. She ws 22 years younger than Catharine Greene. During her lifetime, Europe became a heavily industrialized continent. But the industry she worked in was still strongly linked to agriculture: to growing grapes for wine. It still is. Without her, however, today's champagne trade would be much smaller and less efficient.

Mary Quant lives in industrialized Britain today. Her clothes and other products are mass-produced (produced in factories). But her career was founded on industrial methods that are much older than the Industrial Revolution; they are as old as agriculture. The dresses that first took her to success were made at home, in a small apartment in London. This book will show you some of the differences between these women and some of the similarities.

American widow Catharine Littlefield Greene (1731–1793), who with inventor Eli Whitney created the cotton gin. This machine completely changed the world's textile industries of the time.

Above, French businesswoman Nicole-Barbe Clicquot who, at the age of 27, took over the family champagne firm in 1804. Under its new name of "Veuve Clicquot" or "Widow Clicquot," the champagne she sold became internationally famous.

Mary Quant, British clothes designer, wearing two of the 1960s accessories she launched; gilt chains and shoulder-bags. "I like being given the credit for such things," she commented. "I want to be first with a whole lot more."

The cotton gin

It worked. The Northerner's new machine worked. The Georgia planters crowded close to watch as the machine's inventor fed his invention with more raw cotton: the upland cotton that grew almost anywhere in the Southern states. It might grow anywhere but, until then, it had been almost useless. Its green, velvety seeds clung to the cotton fibers as if they'd been glued. And it took a whole day for a worker to clean a single pound.

Eli Whitney grasped the machine's handle and started turning. Peering intently, the planters saw its tiny hooks flash as they caught the cotton up. They heard the bristling noise as the rows of brushes swept it free of the hooks. The seeds, caught and held by the machinery as the cotton swept through, had gone. What came out was clean, fluffy fiber, ready to pack and sell.

The men turned delightedly to their hostess, Catharine Greene, who'd invited them to see the new invention. She'd been quite right. As she had promised, Eli Whitney really could make anything. What she and he had done, that spring of 1793, was to make the South's fortune. The United States of America was then a very new country. The Americans had only declared their independence from Britain 17 years before, in

Above, Eli Whitney, as he was in the 1820s. After graduating from Yale University in 1792, he planned to become a children's tutor in South Carolina. But, during the journey, he met Catharine Greene of Georgia. She invited him to stay at Mulberry Grove, where she introduced him to the cotton planters.

Left, cotton in its raw state: a "boll" of American cotton, with the seeds hidden in the fluffy white fibers.

1776. Britain would make them pay a high price for it: six years of war, followed by poverty and chaos.

Things became especially difficult for farmers in the Southern states. In the pre-war days, they had made good livings out of growing rice, tobacco and the dye-plant called indigo. But war and neglect had wrecked the carefully-drained paddy fields where the rice grew. The heavy tobacco crops had wrecked the soil itself. As for indigo, Europe had now found a cheaper source of supply, in the Far East.

But there was one ray of hope: cotton. The worried plantation owners of the Southern states knew that the North wanted cotton. In 1789, an Englishman named Sam Slater had arrived in Rhode Island and set up a cotton-spinning mill. Its machines were copies of the ones that had been invented in Britain earlier that century. Slater had smuggled the details out in his head.

The USA now had a cotton industry, and the British mills wanted cotton, too. But what was the good of that? One sort of cotton, with black seeds, could be cleaned easily. But it only grew on the coast. Green-seed cotton, which everyone could grow, was full of those obstinate green seeds.

In November 1792, Catharine Greene played hostess to a group of Georgia neighbors, friends of her dead husband. They were full of their worries over money and cotton. Catharine Greene was herself the mistress of a big estate, called Mulberry Grove, so she understood their problems. Her comfortable house was always full of guests, George Washington himself had visited her, but the comfort hid a long string of debts. Listening to the anxious planters, she had a suggestion to make. They should take their problems to another of her visitors: Eli Whitney from Massachussets, who had come South to teach a neighbor's children.

Now, just six months later, the answer to the planters' worries stood before them: the "cotton gin." Its inven-

tor had built it on the spot, right here in Mulberry Grove's basement. The tiny hooks were of wire borrowed from Catharine's daughter; it was meant for a birdcage she had never made. Catharine herself had invented the idea of the machine's brushwork. When Whitney could not decide how to clean off the machine's teeth, she'd told him to use her hearth brush. The machine would clean cotton ten times faster than anything the planters had ever tried before. And it was called the cotton engine, or "cotton gin."

The birthplace of the Industrial Revolution in the USA: the cotton mill that Sam Slater built in Rhode Island to house English-style spinning machines.

The British connection

The rattling noise filled the street in front of the Georgia courthouse. The people waiting on its steps looked up, then grinned and nodded at each other. Upstairs in a nearby building, a gin was working, turning the fluffy bolls of cotton into wealth for the planter who'd built it.

The noise grew louder; another gin had been set going. The men outside grinned wider, gesturing at the courthouse door. Somewhere inside, that Northerner Whitney was making a plea to the judge; demanding money from people who'd used the gin. But he was never going to find them. No one in Georgia was going to say they'd seen a gin at work, and hearing didn't count as seeing. Serves him right, said the Georgia bystanders. Serves him right for his money-grubbing impudence. The cotton was theirs, not his. He had no right to get rich on it.

When, a few years before, Whitney produced the machine he and Catharine had created, he thought it would make him rich. So did his partner, Phineas Miller. Miller, another Northerner, was Catharine Greene's estate manager. In 1796 he became her husband. The partners planned to build cotton gins and use them to clean the green-seed cotton the planters grew. For payment, they would take two-fifths of the cotton they cleaned. Until they were making a profit, Catharine promised to back them by lending them money from the Mulberry Grove estate. Then she let some of the estate be sold off to meet the partners' bills.

But the plans made at Mulberry Grove didn't work out. The gin was easy to copy, even by people who'd never seen it. By patenting his invention, Whitney had tried to protect it. By law, other people would now be forbidden to copy its design. But the Georgia planters built their own "pirate" gins. Bypassing the law like this didn't bother them. They had too much to lose if they obeyed it.

What they risked losing was the chance of selling cotton to Britain. By this time, British inventions like Hargreaves' Spinning Jenny and Arkwright's Water Frame had revolutionized the process of spinning cotton thread, or yarn. With the help of these new machines, yarn production had shot up — and this yarn could be woven into smooth, silky cloth rather than the coarse textiles that hand-spun yarn produced. Europe's population was growing, and all the extra people needed clothes to wear. Cotton cloth — light, strong, easily washed — would give them what they wanted. Until the 1780s, it had been expensive. Only the rich could buy the delicate cotton fabrics that merchants brought from India. But now, thanks to the spinning machines, the price could come down.

Demand for cheap cotton cloth rose. Demand for raw cotton to feed the machines rose as well. Supplies already came from India and the Caribbean, but these weren't enough. Britain wanted more and more. It was the promise of making huge sums by selling cotton to Britain that had given the planters of Georgia new hope.

Whitney, Miller and Catharine Greene were responding to that hope when they produced the cotton gin, publicized it, and launched the new service on the market. But they made the mistake of charging too much for a process that was basically very simple. The cotton growers, frantic to meet Britain's demands, took a short cut around the problem. They didn't buy the service offered. They stole it.

The cotton gin, invented at Mulberry Grove. This is the miniature model that Whitney made for the US Patent Office.

One of the British inventions that revolutionized the cotton-spinning process; Samuel Crompton's spinning mule: here seen in a British factory of the late 18th century.

❝ WITNESS

"In one instance I had great difficulty to prove that the machine had been used in Georgia and at the same moment there were three separate sets of this machinery in motion [within] 50 yards of the building in which the court sat and all so near that the rattling was distinctly heard on the steps of the courthouse."
Source: Eli Whitney, (quoted in *The World of Eli Whitney*).

"Now cotton yarn is cheaper than linen yarn; and cotton goods are very much used in place of cambrics, lawns and other expensive fabrics of flax; and they have almost totally superceded the silks. Women in all ranks from the highest to the lowest, are clothed in British manufactures of cotton, from the muslin cap on the crown of the head to the cotton stockings under the sole of the foot."
Source: British observer, 1806 (quoted in *The Industrial Revolution*

Fontana Economic History of Europe, ed C. M. Cipolla, 1973).

"The skill and energy applied to the cultivation of cotton in the United States have enabled that country to distance all others in providing a supply for the manufactures of England."
Source: Edward Baines, writing in *The History of the Cotton Manufacture*, c.1828.

Slave labor

The gins Whitney heard rattling outside the Georgia courthouse were being worked by black slaves. But they were not allowed to bear witness in a Southern courtroom so Whitney could not use their evidence to help him. To the white planters, slaves weren't people like themselves. They were possessions to be bought, sold and used.

North America had been importing slaves from Africa since early in the 17th century. By the end of the 18th century, several of the new Northern states had banned slavery. But it still survived in the South, where large numbers of workers were needed to grow plantation crops like sugar, tobacco and rice. Mulberry Grove, for example, was principally a rice-growing plantation.

When Catharine and her husband, General Greene,

first came there in 1785, they found the plantation's drainage system had been badly damaged by neglect. But, with the slave labor he had bought even before moving into his Georgia home, the General worked fast to repair it. By the following spring, the repairs had been made, and his 130 slaves had planted 190 acres of rice and corn. They also tended the other crops that Mulberry Grove produced. "We have green peas almost fit to eat, and as fine lettuce as ever you saw", General Greene wrote to a friend.

The General died soon afterwards. By this time, the value of the South's rice and tobacco crops was slipping. Without Britain's demand for cotton, and without the gin that made green-seed cotton usable, Southerners might have changed to other ways of making money. But Whitney's invention changed things completely.

WITNESS

"God knows that my will was good enough to have wrung his neck; or to have drained from his heartles system its last drop of blood! And yet I was obliged to turn a deaf ear to her cries for assistance, which to this day ring in my ears. Strong and athletic as I was, no hand of mine could be raised in her defense, but at the peril of both our lives."
Source: Former slave Austin Steward, remembering how his sister was whipped (source published in 1861; quoted in *The Slave Community* by John W. Blassinghame; OUP/NY, 1972).

"A moral, social and political wrong."
Source: Abraham Lincoln on slavery.

At a slave sale, an auctioneer in Virginia invites offers from local planters. Slaves were not allowed to marry. If their masters decided to sell them, slave families were split up. This happened to one couple out of every three.

Left, directed by the white overseer, male and female slaves pick upland or green-seed cotton on a riverside Georgia plantation.

Above, slaves load cotton on to mule carts. Here, the overseer is giving his directions from horseback: an important sign of his power.

Cotton was a crop that demanded huge amounts of care. Seed had to be sown in the spring, and the plantation fields kept clear of weeds and sapling trees. Picking started in late summer, and could go on to Christmas and beyond. All this work was done by hand; that was what the slaves were used for. They were also used for all the ordinary farm work, like mending fences. The slaves also kept the plantation-owner's home going, they cooked meals, looked after the children and waited on the adults. They were essential to the production of cotton.

In the first 50 years of the 19th century, the number of slaves owned in the South climbed from about 800,000 to four million. The cotton-growing industry had revived slavery.

Together, slavery and cotton created wealth for the whites of the Southern states. If a Southern planter had money to spare, he'd use it to buy more land and more slaves to work it. But in the North, where slavery was banned, people used their spare money for something else: they invested it in industry. They lent it to businessmen who wanted to build new factories, or to companies to build new roads, canals or railroads.

By 1860, the North had become a rich industrial region. The South had stayed what it had always been: an enormous farm. Resentfully, the South bought the North's industrial goods, but refused to start up industries of its own. But soon the Southerners would realize they'd made an enormous mistake.

"King Cotton"

Crash! On April 12, 1861, Fort Sumter in Charleston Harbor shook with the sound of firing. For two days, the guns of the Southern states would pound against it before the troops inside gave in. Neither side knew it, but they were fighting the first battle of the American Civil War: the war between the North and the South.

The war lasted for four years, until 1865. In the end, the North won. A million Americans were wounded, and over half of them died. The war started because seven of the Southern states decided to leave the Union. (Four more later joined them.) But, from the point of view of many Southerners, it was really fought about slavery — and cotton.

The rebel states left the Union because they feared the anti-slavery states of the North would ban slavery in the South as well. That would mean the end of both the Southerners' wealth and their whole way of life. It would mean the end of the "Cotton Kingdom."

The "Cotton Kingdom" as it was in 1860, just before the Civil War started. At that time, the USA contained fewer states than it does now.

This kingdom was an enormous one. From the Atlantic, it stretched 1,500 miles to the west, taking in all the warm, moist areas where green-seed cotton would grow. And the stubborn green seeds themselves were now no problem. The kingdom had over 25,000 gins for cleaning its cotton crop.

The amount of cotton that the South and its slaves produced grew with lightning speed. The year before Whitney arrived at Mulberry Grove, the USA exported only 18,000 lbs. of cotton. In 1793, the year the cotton gin was launched, exports stood at 487,000 lbs. In 1794, they more than doubled. By 1820, the annual total had soared to 127,000,000 lbs. or 400,000 bales. In 1860, the number of bales the USA exported almost reached the four million mark. The 1860 total accounted for two-thirds of all the goods that the USA sold abroad. Its most important customer was still Britain, birthplace of the Industrial Revolution and now the greatest industrial country in the world.

The British got rich, and so did some Americans. But Whitney didn't. In the end, he defeated the farmers who had "stolen" his invention, but he only made $90,000 from the cotton gin, and he should have made millions. Miller, who died in 1803, didn't get rich either. Nor did Catharine Greene. The cotton gin made her money worries worse, not better. Mulberry Grove, had to be sold off at a bargain price in 1800. Later Whitney himself helped pay some of her bills.

A few of the Southern planters made a lot of money. The thousand or so families who owned a hundred slaves or more used the wealth their slaves created for them to support a leisured, luxurious lifestyle that stressed elegant manners and pursuits such as riding and hunting. They hated the alertness and bustle of the industrialized North. But it was the North that made their machinery, the North that organized the sales of their cotton abroad, and the North that lent them money if they needed it. So the North got some of the cotton wealth as well: almost half, the Southerners complained.

The reason the South went to war in 1861 was also the reason why the Georgia planters had cheated Whitney out of his money. It had too much to lose. After four years of appalling fighting, it lost the war instead. It did not have the guns, the supplies, or the money of the Northern states, and Britain, its great customer, refused to help. Instead, the British sold boots, woollen cloth and steel . . . to the North.

Left, an ocean-going ship takes cotton on board at Savannah, Georgia. The South's transportation links with its customers were vital to the cotton trade. When the North stopped ships leaving and entering Southern ports during the Civil War, the value of the South's cotton exports dropped form $191m, to $4m.

Right, the bombardment of Fort Sumter in Charleston Harbor on April 12, 1861 marked the beginning of the American Civil War.

At Mulberry Grove

Urgently, Catharine Greene leant forward across the dining table. "Try again," she said. "My dear friend, do not be cast down; I beg you, try again."

Obedient to his hostess, Eli Whitney turned the gin's handle. Round went the toothed roller with its wire hooks; and round, caught on the hooks, went the raw cotton. The seeds came out, caught on the slatted breastwork fixed above the roller. But then the cleaned cotton went round again — and again. It would not come off the teeth that held it. With every turn of the handle, they collected more cotton still.

Whitney grunted with effort. The handle, which had turned so easily a minute ago, was now seizing up. A second more, and it stuck completely. Inside the machine, everything was in disorder. A horrible tangle of cotton bolls, dry cotton husks, and cleaned cotton had brought the roller to a halt.

There was a dismal silence. Frowning, Catharine Greene stared at the heap of cotton on her dining table, and the little model it surrounded. Things were as bad as Mr. Whitney had said. She hadn't believed him when, half an hour ago, he'd told them that he could go no further. Phineas Miller hadn't believed him either. Nor had her lawyer, Judge Pendleton, who was spending the evening with them. The judge had been part of the scheme from the start, several weeks ago. He had been one of the men who'd been complaining about the green-seed cotton, the day she had re-commended Mr. Whitney's talents.

Today, the judge had been blunt when he'd heard the bad news. "Fiddlesticks, my dear sir," he had said. "We have every confidence in your abilities: every confidence in the world. Do you not have the trust of our gracious, our wise, hostess?" He bowed teasingly to Catharine, who laughed and tapped him with her fan. "Have your new engine brought up here," he went on, "and let us see what plagues you so."

They had now seen it. They had seen it all too clearly. Whitney's machine cleaned the cotton of its seeds. But he couldn't think of a way to remove the de-seeded cotton from the toothed roller.

It was Phineas Miller who broke the silence first. "My good Whitney," he said. "Mrs. Greene is right. Let us not be down-hearted. Let us persevere. Let us con-sider: now, according to scientific principles . . ." his

Catharine, often called "Caty," Greene. This picture is the only portrait of her that survives. It shows her in middle age, when she had been twice widowed. She didn't like it.

voice died away as he gazed thoughtfully at the machine. Catharine glanced at him with gratitude. Yes, that was the way to keep up Mr Whitney's spirits. He was a practical man, and he wanted practical suggestions. Dear Phineas; how often it happened that he seemed to read her mind, and other people's too. How glad she was she had decided to become Mrs. Miller. Affectionately, she brushed a stray wisp of cotton off her fiancé's shoulders. Then, suddenly at-tentive, she stared at the wisp as she rubbed it be-tween her fingers.

"WITNESS

The way it might have happened: Whitney turns the model gin's handle, while Catharine Greene cleans its toothed roller with a hearth brush. This reconstruction was drawn for an American magazine in 1878.

With Judge Pendleton hovering over them, Whitney and Miller cleaned the machine's roller, adjusted its workings, tried it out. The adjustment made no difference. They tried again. It still didn't work. The next attempt wrenched some of the teeth out of the roller. Red-faced and wretched, Whitney looked up. "Mrs. Greene," he stammered. "I — I fear . . ."

Firmly, his hostess interrupted him. "Mr. Whitney," she said. "Your roller is like a suit of clothes. All it needs is a brush." She glanced round the room; then, with skirts rustling, she hurried over to the hearth and returned with the hearth brush. "Turn the handle again," she commanded, and held the brush steady alongside the toothed roller.

The brush's bristles were soft. They brushed some of the cotton off the roller, but not much. "Oh, the blasted thing!" Catharine cried, and threw the brush on the floor. But Whitney looked like a man who'd seen a vision. There was another silence. "Thank you, thank you for the hint," he said at last. "I have it now."

CATHARINE GREEN

In the public eye

As a young wife, Catharine Greene had followed her husband through the campaigns of America's War of Independence. Like the rest of the army she spent the winters in snow-bound huts. But, by laughing off her cold and hunger, she boosted everyone's morale, and won the lifelong friendship of General George Washington himself. Later, she also turned Eli Whitney into a life-long friend, and for the same reason.

By nature, she was a sociable, warm-hearted woman, with a gift for inspiring enthusiasm and self-confidence in others. She also had a gift for management.

For people of her time, there was no sharp divide between home and work. Work, the production of wealth, was something that most people did at home, often with their families as the workforce. The cotton gin was a technological breakthrough that helped to power the Industrial Revolution. But, to start with, it was also a home-made contraption, made in the Mulberry Grove basement out of household materials.

Running a modern industry and running a big estate involves the same sort of managerial skills. Although she employed a manager of her own, Catharine Greene possessed many of these skills herself. When Whitney

first joined the long guest-list at Mulberry Grove, there was little to show he was a mechanical genius. But his hostess spotted his potential within a few weeks. She also spotted a problem that she thought he could solve, and she wasted no time in bringing Whitney and the planters together.

While Whitney was working on his invention, Catharine Greene and Miller gave him everything he needed: a home, a workshop, company, advice and privacy from meddling intruders. (A modern firm would treat its research team in much the same way.) Then, when the gin was ready, Catharine ran something very like a modern publicity program. She talked about it, worked up local interest, invited influential friends to see how it worked.

She also helped pay for it. As a planter's widow, she owned a lot of property and, unusually for that time, she kept control of it when she re-married. She was always ready to lend the struggling business money and, when bankruptcy threatened the partners, she came to their help. She let none of these worries spoil her interest in the gin, or her friendship for its main inventor. For many years, people have doubted whether she really helped invent as well as promote

An early example of the world of Catharine Greene: sophisticated, elegant, very sociable. Both before and after the War of Independence, wealthy Americans loved to fill their big houses with guests.

the cotton gin. The part she played in its design has usually been thought of, not as a fact, but as a story: almost a legend. One of the reasons for this is that Whitney never said anything about it. But there were a lot of things Whitney never mentioned and other people, writing not long after the event, did record it. Without Catharine Greene, the gin would never have come into being. She was certainly its midwife; in one way, it seems sure that she was also its co-inventor.

Other homes, in another country, a hundred or so years later; the poverty of English cotton workers in Manchester after the American Civil War blocked the Cotton Kingdom's exports.

WITNESS

"A lady who is superior to the little foibles of her sex, who disdains affectations, who thinks and acts as she pleases, within the limits of virtue and good sense, without consulting the world about it, is generally an object of envy and distraction. Such is Lady Greene. . . . She has a infinite fund of vivacity, the world calls it levity. She possesses an unbounded benevolence. . . . the world calls it imprudence. In short she is honest and unaffected enough to confess that she is a woman, and it seems to me the world dislikes her for nothing else."
Source: Georgia politician Isaac Briggs, who met Catharine Greene in 1785 (quoted in *Caty*).

BIOGRAPHY

1755 Born Catharine Littlefield, on Block Island, Rhode Island.
1774 Marries Nathanael Greene, soon to become a leading commander in the US War of Independence. Later has five children.
1777–8 Joins her husband at the revolutionary force's winter camps.
1785 Moves to Mulberry Grove, a gift to General Greene from the new state of Georgia.
1786 Widowed; makes Phineas Miller, formerly the children's tutor, her estate manager.
1792 Meets Eli Whitney, hired by Miller as children's tutor for a friend. Invites him to Mulberry Grove; introduces him to the planters and the cotton-seed problem. Inspires and encourages the invention of the cotton-gin.
1793 Publicizes the model gin amongst her friends. Several working gins are later set up at Mulberry Grove.
1795 Pledges the funds of the Greene estate to back the Whitney/Miller partnership.
1796 Marries Phineas Miller.
1800 Mulberry Grove sold; the family moves to Dungeness.
1803 Widowed for the second time.
1807 Meets Whitney for the last time.
1814 Dies, aged 59.

CHAMPAGNE BOOM

The Widow takes over

She was going to run the business herself. Philippe Clicquot was so amazed that, for a second, he forgot his grief. He stared at his daughter-in-law, sitting before him in her high-waisted black dress. It was unbelievable. She was only 27; she knew nothing of commerce; she had a baby to tend to. Her heart ought to be in the grave, with her dead husband François. Yet here she was, a few weeks later, saying she would run her husband's champagne firm.

Calmly, Nicole-Barbe Clicquot stared back at him. "Naturally," she said, "we will trade under a different name. I have decided what it will be. I am the head of the firm, so it will be called after me: Widow Clicquot. We will trade as Veuve Clicquot Ponsardin and Company."

It was Philippe who had originally founded the firm in 1772. Not long before, the monarchs and aristocrats of 18th-century Europe had discovered they loved a drink that came from the Champagne district of France: sparkling champagne. It was difficult to produce, and trade was limited. In 1785, for example, only 300,000 bottles were sold. But, small though the champagne industry was, several firms were still able to prosper: Ruinart, Moët, Lanson . . . and Clicquot.

But then, in October 1805, François Clicquot fell ill with fever at the family home in Reims. Within a fortnight, he was dead. Dazed with shock and sorrow, his elderly father decided there was no point in going on. He was starting to close the firm down when, to his astonishment, the young widow announced that she was taking over. She borrowed money from her father, Monsieur Ponsardin, who was a rich textile merchant. She won over old Monsieur Clicquot, who lent her more. And, within four months of François' death, the firm of Widow Clicquot & Company was in business.

The people of Reims were probably not too shocked at the idea. At that time in France, the division between home and work was as blurred as it was in Catharine Greene's America. The division between industry (or making goods) and commerce (selling them) was also a blurred one.

It was quite common for French women of the early 1800s to run family firms, do the books, and make technical decisions. Sometimes they worked with their husbands or male relatives; sometimes on their own. Madame Clicquot decided she was too inexperienced

to work on her own, so she looked for help elsewhere. Champagne is unlike most other wines in two important ways. The first one is obvious: it fizzes! It gets its fizz, or "sparkle," from a long and complex manufacturing process. The other thing that makes champagne different is what goes into it. Unlike most other wines, it's made by blending the produce of different vineyards. Creating the right blend is as difficult as creating a work of art.

When Madame Clicquot took over, the blending operation was just as skilled as it is now. The manufacturing process was even longer. Soon, she would work out a way of speeding up the whole operation. Soon, too, she would hire her own skilled blender. But, at first, she got another firm to do the blending work for her.

She also made her husband's star salesman, Monsieur Bohne, a partner in her new company. She never regretted her choice; he helped her, advised her, bullied her to improve the quality of her product, and sold it for her right across Europe.

To help them, they had both their own sales team and another, much bigger one: the armies who were then turning all Europe into a battlefield.

Below, picking grapes in a vineyard in 1801. The deep basket carried by the women is called a "mannequin." Nearly 2,000 years before, the Ancient Romans had used grape baskets that looked exactly the same.

Above, the height of luxury: aristocrats of the 18th century drink a toast in sparkling champagne. This scene has been carved out of the solid chalk that lies below the soil of the champagne district.

  **WITNESS**

"The dinner was a frolic of seven young men, who bespoke it to the utmost extent of expense; one article was a tart made of Duke cherries from a hot-house, and another that they tasted but one glass out of each bottle of champagne."

Source: British politician Horace Walpole, describing a luxury dinner-party in 1751.

"Shower on him all the good things and pleasures that Reims and the neighborhood can offer. Take possession of him entirely. Do not let him have a second to himself. Either you or your friends invite him for every meal so that our competitors never get near him."

Source: Monsieur Bohne, advising Madame Clicquot on how to treat a customer (quoted in *Madame Clicquot: Her Peaceful Conquest of Russia*, by Count Bertrand de Vogüé, published by Veuve Clicquot-Ponsardin, 1982).

"The Queen of Reims."
Source: Nicole-Barbe Clicquot's nickname in the Champagne district.

"One quality: the finest"
Source: the motto of Nicole-Barbe Clicquot.

France at war

When, in 1799, young Mademoiselle Ponsardin of Reims married François Clicquot, the wedding was held in a champagne cellar. Both had been born Roman Catholics but some churches had not yet been re-opened for Catholic worship. They had been closed by the revolutionaries who had run France since 1789.

During the last ten years of the 18th century, France was plunged in turmoil. Sections of the middle classes and the poor rebelled against the harsh way they were ruled. Fired by their motto, "Liberty, equality, fraternity," they overthrew the government.

The revolutionaries sent thousands of their enemies to the guillotine, including the French king himself. To protect the gains they had made during the Revolution, they went to war against Austria, Britain and Spain. They ruthlessly hunted down members of the old ruling class, but they did not outlaw the luxuries the aristocrats once enjoyed. Instead, they enjoyed them themselves, champagne included. Revolutionary leader Georges Danton even bathed in it.

In 1796, the revolutionary government put a young Corsican officer in charge of a force that would attack Austria through Italy. His name was Napoleon Bonaparte. He became so successful that eight years later, in 1804, he crowned himself Emperor of the French. Thanks to the might of his armies, he also controlled the Low Countries (present-day Belgium, Luxembourg and the Netherlands), and part of Italy. Soon he would control much more, from Spain to the Russian border. But Britain held out against him.

Jean-Remy Moët, head of the biggest champagne firm, welcomes his emperor and friend, Napoleon, to the Moët headquarters in Epernay. The Emperor stayed with Monsieur Moët many times, the last one in 1814.

WITNESS

"All is going very badly. I have been busy for several days walling up my cellars, but I am afraid that this will not stop me from being robbed and pillaged. Well, if I am ruined, I am, and I must resign myself to it and to working for a living. I shall not regret losing my comfortable life except for my child, since it should have happened five or six years earlier and then she would not have known the enjoyments which she is losing. This will certainly be painful."
Source: Nicole-Barbe Clicquot, writing to a cousin in 1814, before the fall of Reims (quoted in *Madame Clicquot: Her Peaceful Conquest of Russia*).

*"When are you off,
You Moscow sot?
You really want
To drink the lot?"*
Source: Popular song in the Champagne district, 1814 (French version quoted in *Champagne*, by Patrick Forbes, published by Gollancz, 1967).

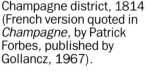

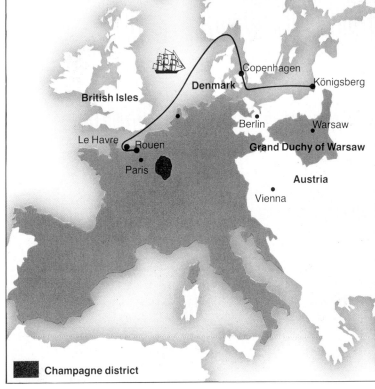

Europe in 1812, showing the area under Napoleon's domination. Also marked is France's champagne district, and the voyage made by Madame Clicquot's agent to smuggle champagne into Russia (see pp. 26–27).

Champagne district

Napoleon's wars often made things difficult for trade. Goods were damaged or delayed. Salesmen, traveling wherever the warring armies would let them pass, had a dismal time. The staff of the champagne industry suffered with the rest. In Copenhagen, one of Madame Clicquot's salesmen was shelled by the British Navy. In Central Europe, another got so tired of camping in peasants' huts that he bought himself a mobile home: a carriage. And, in Amsterdam, their firm lost a whole shipment of 50,000 bottles, with the British Navy again being to blame.

But these were small problems compared to the gains that Napoleon brought the traders of France. His armies had turned most of Europe into a sort of French colony. Within this huge area, people followed French laws, adopted French tastes, and bought French goods. The roving champagne salesmen found their Emperor had done all the really hard work for them.

Their luck went on holding even when the Emperor's own fortunes started to fail. But things looked bad at first, for the Champagne district lay right on the path that Napoleon's enemies took when they invaded France in 1814. Troops from Austria, Prussia and Russia all poured in to attack the Emperor. Reims itself was captured and re-captured several times. During the fighting, Napoleon stayed both with Madame Clicquot's brother and with the head of the Moët champagne firm in neighbouring Epernay. Then, at last, the allied armies took Reims back again, and held it.

The occupying forces collected harsh taxes and fines from the French population. The officers wallowed in the luxury drink that the conquered territory produced. And the soldiers looted their way through the cellars. But the champagne industry realized that there might be a bright side to the picture. The Russians and the rest were starting a habit that, with luck and good sales management, they would take home with them. It made sense, the manufacturers agreed, to let the armies drink their fill of champagne. They would pay for it later.

The French Revolution did not harm champagne's popularity. This cartoon jeers at "Barrel Mirabeau," brother of one of the Revolution's leaders. He was said to drink two bottles with every meal.

Champagne conquest

There was no bed for Monsieur Bohne in his cabin on board the ship *Gebroeders*. But there were bedbugs: huge ones. As he wrote to his partner in June 1814, they were a good two inches long. All the same, he was cheerful.

Below him, in the hold of the ship, was a large consignment of Veuve Clicquot champagne. Russia was still at war with France. Russian people were forbidden to buy French exports. But, all the same, he and Madame Clicquot were planning to get ahead of their rival manufacturers. They planned to smuggle a shipload of champagne right into the empire of the Czar himself. By getting there before anyone else, Monsieur Bohne could sell his smuggled goods at a high price.

When he reached Königsberg (now Kaliningrad), in what was then Prussia, he heard the Russians had lifted their ban. Back home in Reims, Madame Clicquot had heard the news earlier. She didn't wait to hear how her agent planned to sell the first shipload. Instead, she sent another one chasing off after him. In eastern Europe, the artful Monsieur Bohne rose brilliantly to the occasion. He sold champagne to a few people; he disappointed many more by saying the rest of his stocks were promised elsewhere. Then he hinted that, if they wanted to pay the earth, he just might be able to find some. . . .

By the time both shiploads reached the Russian capital, the price of Veuve Clicquot champagne had gone through the roof. From then on, the fortunes of the firm were made. The Russians could drink all the "Klikoskoe" that Monseiur Bohne could sell, and more. Even at modest meals, as poet Alexander Pushkin once phrased it, "the champagne flowed like water."

But Madame Clicquot and her partner weren't the only people to supply the eager Russians. The Ruinarts, oldest of the champagne firms, and the enormous Moët company did big business there as well. Nor was Russia the only market that interested them and their rivals. There was the rest of Europe; there was the young USA. Above all, there was France's former enemy, Britain.

By 1839, Moët & Chandon was selling champagne to society leaders all over the world. They included Queen Victoria, the kings of Greece and Belgium, Russian and German princes, British dukes, Portuguese marquises, Hungarian counts, American bankers, the Lord Mayor of London, and the Bishop of Derry. The market was so profitable that more and more champagne firms sprang up.

In 1844, the industry started to keep figures of how many bottles were sold every year. The first annual total was 6,500,000. The champagne-makers had come a long way since the pre-Revolutionary days, when their output had been measured only in thousands. The champagne salesmen had worked hard, but so had the production teams. It was up to them to make sure that their output was big enough to meet the demand that the salesmen created.

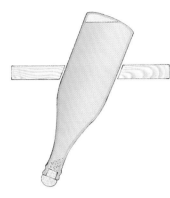

"To remove this sediment and to render the wines marketable, those of the best quality are decanted clear into fresh bottles in about fifteen or eighteen months when the wine is perfected. A certain loss, amounting to one or two bottles in a dozen, is sustained by their explosion previous to this last stage. Another process is sometimes adopted for getting rid of the sediment without the trouble of decanting in this mode; the bottles are reserved in a frame proper for the purpose . . . so as to permit the foulness to fall into the neck; while in this position the cork is dexterously withdrawn and that portion of the wine which is foul, allowed to escape."
Source: J. MacCulloch, *Remarks on the Art of Making Wine,* 1821. MacCulloch visited the champagne houses around 1815, and saw *remuage* being practiced.

One of the newer firms, Mumm, had brought in huge new vats in which to do its blending. Madame Clicquot herself had invented a method of removing the sediment from the blended champagne without re-bottling it (see diagram). And the firms hurried to use a newly-invented instrument for measuring the sugar content of the wine: a step that reduced the enormous number of bottles that exploded while their contents matured.

In 1853, the total of bottles sold reached 10 million. By 1868, they had jumped up to 15 million. The following year, the song "*Champagne Charlie*" became the hit of the British music-halls: "Moët and Chandon", as the British sang, "is the wine for me." By 1871, the sales total had jumped yet again, to 20 million, and it would go on rising.

In less than a century, champagne had conquered the world. And its empire would last, unlike that of the Emperor who had acted as one of its salesmen.

How *remuage* works. Turning a bottle upside down makes the sediment – or solid waste material in the wine – drift down towards the cork. The process is done in stages: the left-hand picture shows an early stage. In the right-hand picture, the process is almost complete. The bottle's temporary cork can soon be removed, along with the sediment resting on top of it. During *remuage*, the bottle rests in a specially-shaped rack, or *pupitre*.

Guests prepare to drink a toast at this magnificent banquet in Austria. There was only drink suitable for such an occasion: champagne, served by waiters like the ones on the left.

Right, in this cellar cut out of the chalk, champagne bottles are stacked on slotted planks for the *remuage* process. The man on the right is taking the sediment out of bottles that the process has cleared.

In the cellars

It was cold down here under the ground. Shivering, Nicole-Barbe Clicquot pulled her shawl more tightly round her shoulders. The long ends irritated her; they got in the way. She seized them, crossed them over, and tied them behind her waist in a firm knot. Then, in the flickering lantern light, she bent over the table with its load of upside-down bottles.

Somewhere up above, the people of Reims were going about their evening business: eating, drinking, laughing, talking. But underground, here in the deepest champagne cellar, everything was quiet. All the workers had finished for the day. There was no one left here but herself, and the rats that rustled in corners. But Madame Clicquot had better things to do than think about rats. The sediment in her wine was making problems for the firm. Night after night for three months, she had been coming down to the cellars to find a solution.

Click-click-click the bottles went, as she rattled them two by two against the wood that held them. Methodically, she worked her way along the table: gripping a bottle in each hand turning it round in its slot, shaking it, tilting it more so that the thick, sticky sediment inside slid down nearer the cork.

There were two tables now; she'd started with only one, lugged down from the kitchen. Each table was bored with rows of slots; each slot held a bottle, standing upside down and on a slant. And each bottle had to be turned, shaken, tilted.

Bang! Somewhere in the darkness beyond the lantern, a bottle had exploded. It was always happening. Sometimes the rats ate through the strings that held the corks. And the bottles were not strong enough anyway. One day, Madame Clicquot thought, someone might discover a way of making stronger glass. Something had to be done: when bottles burst, cellarmen were sometimes blinded by the flying splinters.

In the old days, before the Revolution, workers were allowed to sell the broken glass and keep the money, but it didn't make up for losing an eye.

Rubbing her aching fingers, she walked over to the other table: the one started three months ago, when she'd finally lost patience with the way things were going. Business was wonderful, orders were rushing in. But, down here in the cellars, the workers couldn't

La grande Dame du Champagne

Madame Veuve Clicquot-Ponsardin

Champagne-maker Nicole-Barbe Clicquot, head of the firm of Veuve Clicquot Ponsardin. Her business motto was "One quality: the finest."

keep up with demand. The reason was always the same: the sediment. Getting rid of it meant re-bottling the wine. And that took time, too much time. But there might be another way. That's what she was doing down here by herself: finding out.

Gingerly, the Widow took a bottle from the three-month table. She held it, still upside down, in front of the lantern. If it broke now. . . . But it didn't. And what was this? Inside, all the sediment was at last sitting at the bottom, on top of the cork. The moment had come. She shifted her grip, putting one finger over the cork. The base of the bottle she held against her stomach, the top pointed at the ground. Then she reached for the cellarman's knife she'd brought with her.

Cut-away diagram of 19th century champagne house, showing some of the manufacturing processes. By now, the sloping *pupitres* (racks) on the right have replaced the slotted planks and tables first used for *remuage*.

The knife slashed through the strings on the cork. With her other arm, Madame Clicquot instinctively swung the bottle upwards. There was a crack, like a gun going off. The cork flew out and the sediment after it. The wine started to froth out, but she swiftly stopped it with her thumb. She peered at the bottle again. Hardly any liquid was lost and, in the soft lantern light, the wine shone crystal clear.

Nicole-Barbe Clicquot smiled with pleasure. But her mind was already racing ahead. How many bottles could someone clear like this in a day? Eight hundred? A thousand? She'd set the men working on it tomorrow. There was only one way to find out. And find out she would.

WITNESS

"What marvellous luck. Heaven overwhelms me with her blessings after all the bad moments which I have been through. A thousand and a thousand thanks to God! It is also a new proof of how clever you have been with the sharing out of the 10,000 bottles. Everywhere wonderful prices and no waste at all."
Source: Nicole-Barbe Clicquot, writing to Monsieur Bohne, after the smuggled wine reaches St Petersburg (quoted in *Madame Clicquot: Her Peaceful Conquest of Russia*).

"You remember last year at this time when I was miserable? I did nothing, I had no hope of doing anything. When the Russians crossed the Rhine, my cup was full. Well, out of all these terrible things was born the good business that I have just done and hope to do again. . . . One just cannot always be unlucky."
Source: Nicole-Barbe Clicquot, in a letter to a cousin, late 1814 (quoted in *Madame Clicquot: Her Peaceful Conquest of Russia*).

In the public eye

When Nicole-Barbe Clicquot took over her dead husband's firm, she was taking over a small family business. Her raw materials were grown on the spot, by peasants who'd been using the same agricultural methods for centuries. And her main business premises, the cellars, were just as old, if not older. They had first been dug out by the Romans, who brought wine-making to the area around AD50.

It was still a family firm when she died in 1866, although the family was that of Edouard Werlé. (His descendants run the business today.) The grapes it processed were still grown in the traditional way and the cellars, too, remained unchanged.

But what went on in them had changed a great deal, and the firm itself wasn't small any longer. Nor was the industry of which it formed a part. By 1866, the Champagne district of France was selling well over 10

million bottles a year of its famous wine, and rich people all over the world were drinking it. It was Madame Clicquot who made a lot of this huge growth possible.

Her invention of *remuage* was only one of her achievements, though an important one. Without it, the champagne-makers would have gone on using their slow, wasteful method of clearing the wine of impurities. That would have meant loss of business, at a time when demand was soaring.

The Widow's real triumph was helping to create that demand.

She recognized and promoted a brilliant salesman, Monsieur Bohne. She was also a gifted saleswoman herself. As shown by the voyage of the *Gebroeders* in 1814 and its follow-up, she could make decisions fast and she was as skilled as her partner at implementing them. When, for instance, she sent off the second shipload of champagne, she made sure that no one would rob her firm of its triumph: she insisted that no other wine should be carried in the ship she chartered.

She was not afraid of taking risks. To help the firm, she was ready to risk her personal property as well. When the war stripped the profits away from her growing business, she kept it going by selling her jewelry. She supervised every process in her cellars with an eagle eye, checking that what came out of them was "one quality: the finest." If something needed changing, change it she would.

When she died, the number of women in industry had fallen dramatically. Industry had stopped being an occupation thought proper for ladies. But the champagne trade managed to remain an exception. There was a "Veuve Heidsieck" as well as a "Veuve Clicquot." The firm of Louis Roederer for a time belonged to Louis's daughter.

Most famous of all was another widow, Louise Pommery. When she took over the firm in 1858, it specialized in the older, more traditional wines of Champagne: still (non-bubbly) ones. She switched production over to sparkling champagne, and then, against all the competition, carved out a strong international market for her new product. Madame Cliquot had set an example that, in one industry at least, the women of the 19th century could follow.

The business headquarters of Veuve Clicquot Ponsardin, in the Rue du Temple in Reims, drawn by a 19th-century English visitor. The firm's offices are still in the Rue du Temple today.

A cellarman of the 1980s carries out *remuage* in the firm's cellars.

BIOGRAPHY

1777 Born Barbe-Nicole Ponsardin. (She changed her name to Nicole-Barbe in adulthood.)
1799 Marries François Clicquot, heir to the wine business started in 1772 by his father.
1803 Has a child, Clementine.
1805 Widowed. Determines to keep the family wine business going. Borrows money from her father and father-in-law, takes Monsieur Bohne into partnership; decides to farm the blending process out to the head of another wine firm, Jérome Fourneaux. Launches the revived firm as "Widow Clicquot Ponsardin, Fourneaux and Company."

1806–1810 With Bohne's help, improves the quality of the firm's champagne, starts winning customers in Eastern Europe and Russia.
1810 Ends link with Fourneaux; employs her own blenders, changes the name of the firm to "Widow Clicquot Ponsardin."
1812 Russia, invaded by Napoleon, bans French imports.
1814 The voyage of the ship *Gebroeders.* Russian sales start soaring. Before 1815 experiments with processing techniques; eventually works out *remuage* system to get rid of sediment without re-bottling. A visitor to her cellars saw this system

being used in 1815.
1817 Arranges the marriage of her daughter to the Count de Chevigné.
1821 Monsieur Bohne dies.
1822 Madame Clicquot branches out into other business activities; she opens a bank in Reims, and also enters the textile industry.
1828 A financial crisis is solved by a junior Clicquot employee, Édouard Werlé. The Clicquot bank and textile business are later closed.
1831 Werlé becomes Widow Clicquot's main partner.
1866 Dies, aged 89.

Bed-sitter factory

The cats were playing with the patterns again. Hurriedly, their owner disentangled them. Without the paper dress patterns, there would be no dresses. Without the dresses, rushed down to the boutique every evening, there would be no boutique. The pattern paper was made from fish-bones, and the cats liked eating it.

There was no way of keeping them out of the workroom. They lived there. So did Mary Quant herself, her bed was somewhere underneath the mound of patterns and materials. It had been a pretty bed-sitting room once. But now it was full of dress-makers, and sewing machines, and lengths of cloth from the department store Harrods, bought that morning with the money made on yesterday's batch of dresses.

In the center of it all, Mary herself worked frantically, altering and re-shaping the paper patterns till they gave the look she wanted. Nobody had seen clothes like the ones she was making now: clothes for young people like herself, people in their twenties, or younger. Mary Quant and her customers were members of an unofficial London club. Outsiders called it the "Chelsea Set": the photographers, actors, TV people, painters and party-goers who had made the King's Road their base. They were sophisticated and unconventional. In other words, they liked being startled and shocked; they liked startling other people too. They liked things that were new.

In 1955, the newest thing they liked on the King's Road was Bazaar. Bazaar was a boutique Mary Quant had started with her boyfriend and another partner. It sold sweaters, hats, scarves, jewelry, and the world's first Mary Quant dresses. From the first day, it had been a huge success, with customers stripping the clothes off the rails as fast as Mary Quant could make them.

For most people in 1959, the election slogan of the British Conservative party "We've never had it so good" was perfectly true. During the 1950s, Britain produced more and more goods every year. There were jobs for almost everyone. Wages went up, and so did people's buying-power. By the end of the 1950s, they had money to buy 20 per cent more goods than they could in 1951.

It was a good time to start a clothes shop. World War II had ended ten years before. The rationing that had kept postwar life dull and dingy had ended too. People felt like spending money, and most of them had money to spend. British industry was booming, and in most places almost everybody could find jobs. A third of the workers were women, including married women. Before the war, very few married women went out to work. By the mid-1950s, almost half of Britain's eight million women workers were married. (The proportion was always rising, because women were getting married younger all the time.)

Married or single, they took the jobs that the booming industries created: they became secretaries, typists, shop-assistants, and factory workers. Most of them, especially the married ones, thought of their jobs just as a way of earning money. Only a tiny number thought of themselves as having a career or were able to go on with one once they had children.

The wages of the married women helped pay for goods that, suddenly, ordinary families could afford: televisions, refrigerators, cars. They also bought clothes, and so did the unmarried ones. By 1959, teenage girls would be spending over a third of their spare money on clothes every week. Not many of them, over the next ten years, would get to wear an original Mary Quant dress. But huge numbers would end up wearing 1960s versions of the "Chelsea Look" that Mary Quant first created in her bed-sitter factory.

WITNESS

"We've got everything we want now. I'm satisfied. I've a fridge, a washer and a television set, and that's all I want in life."
Source: English housewife, aged 33, from Newcastle (quoted in *The Fifties*, John Montgomery; Allen & Unwin, 1965).

"I didn't think of myself as a designer. I just knew I wanted to concentrate on finding the right clothes for the young to wear and the right accessories to go with them. . . . The trouble was that when it came to stocking the shop and keeping it stocked, I couldn't find the things I wanted. I decided I would have to try and make these things myself."
Source: Mary Quant in her autobiography, *Quant by Quant*, G. P. Putnam's Sons NY, 1966.

Above, for these British schoolgirls of the 1950s, things to spend their money on include a magazine aimed at precisely their age-group; "Honey," with its teenage readership.

Right, hold-up in Bazaar's windows, with Mary Quant checking the effect. "We had to be arrogant then," she wrote afterwards. "We had to make a sharp, shocking statement at the beginning to be noticed at all."

The new young rich

Only a few young people, most of them Londoners, heard about Bazaar when it first opened. But almost everybody in the country knew about something else that happened in 1955. That was the year that rock 'n' roll really hit Britain.

It came with the film *Rock Around the Clock*, starring US dance-band leader Bill Haley. Right across the country, its pounding beat sent young movie-goers crazy. They tore out the seats in the movie theaters and danced in the space they'd made. Some theaters refused to show the film and older people everywhere reacted with shocked amazement.

The early kings of rock, like Haley and Elvis Presley, revolutionized popular music throughout the West. For many people, both old and young, the arrival of the new music seemed to mark the start of something else. They became aware that a social revolution was going on, too: a revolution that would change the lives of everyone in their teens and early 20s.

Until then, young people had just been people who were younger and poorer versions of their parents. But, starting around the mid-Fifties, they became "teenagers." The music, clothes and activities British teenagers enjoyed were suddenly quite different from the things their parents liked. There was a spirit of rebellion in the air.

Making their own music: a British "skiffle" group of the mid-1950s.

There was nothing new about young people rebelling against their elders. What had changed was their power to make their rebellion felt. They now had the money to pay for it.

In the 1930s, it had been hard to find a job. But now it was easy. The wages teenagers earned were increasing twice as fast as the wages of adults. And teenagers now had twice as much money to spend as they had before the war.

By the end of the 1950s, there were five million of these newly-rich consumers in Britain. Some of them weren't teengers at all. "Teenager" was a useful label to hang on a group of people who were both young and unmarried; you could count as a teenager up to the age of 25!

On average, young women earned less than men. But, between them, they were spending £830 million a year on goods like clothes, cosmetics, drinks and meals out, records, and motorbikes. For manufacturers of all these products, teenagers were now important customers. The way to make money was to produce things they liked: music that was fast and exciting, food that was tasty and easy to eat, clothes that didn't look like what their parents wore.

In 1955, the London *Evening Standard* ran a fashion story that asked: "Why does everyone look like Kelly?" But film star Grace Kelly, with her neat white gloves and sleek blond hair, summed up the way an adult Fifties woman wanted to look. She wanted to look elegant, expensively-dressed, fashionable.

Teenage girls wanted to look fashionable, too. But they also wanted clothes that were comfortable, fun, and cheap. More and more of them, as the Fifties came to an end, wanted to look something like the girls Mary Quant was drawing in her Chelsea workroom. These had sleek hair, too, but it was cut short in a "little girl" bob. Their clothes were like a schoolgirl's uniform, but much shorter than any dress a real schoolgirl was allowed to wear. Instead of the high stiletto heels worn by the 1950s filmstars, a real "Chelsea girl" wore boots, or else little low-heeled slippers worn with coloured stockings. To demonstrate clothes like these, their creator had even invented a completely new sort of fashion parade. In 1957, she'd electrified an audience in St. Moritz by making her models drop their usual elegant pace. To show off their red stockings and flannel pinafores, they ran, skipped and pranced instead.

No one's mother looked like this. It was a perfect type of outfit for many young women who, for the first time in history, had money to spend on themselves exactly as they wished. Mary Quant herself didn't like the word "uniform." But, in the Sixties the look she had created became the uniform of the new teenage culture.

Biba, in Kensington Church Street was owned by designer Barbara Hulanicki. She thought the stylish clothes of the '60s were too expensive for many young women to buy. So Biba fashions were very cheap indeed. When the first Biba boutique opened in 1964, it sold long dresses, made in T-shirt jersey, for the unbelievable price of £2. (The average weekly wage for a Biba customer was about £12.)

WITNESS

"I sit in coffee bars, I wear tight-fitting clothes, and have several friends owning motorcycles. There is nothing wrong with these three things, and it is about time that people realized that the majority of teenagers are as good as, and in some ways better than, those of twenty years ago. I am proud of being a teenager. . . . We can't get the world into a worse mess than the adults have."
Source: 1950s English schoolgirl (quoted in *The Fifties*).

"Young people have now, probably for the first time in our history, obtained freedom of action and the economic strength to rebel against any features in the social structure which displease them. They can no longer be ignored."
Source: Professor J. B. Mays, writing in *The Young Pretenders*, Michael Joseph, 1965.

"Good designers . . . know that to have any influence they must keep in step with public needs . . . public opinion . . . They must catch the spirit of the day and interpret it in clothes before other designers begin to twitch at the nerve ends. I just happened to start when that 'something in the air' was coming to the boil. The clothes I made happened to fit in exactly with the teenage trend, with pop records and espresso bars and jazz clubs."
Source: Mary Quant, in her autobiography.

Below, the "Mods," or "Moderns," were the style setters that most male teenagers of the 60s ended up copying. As Mary Quant commented shortly afterwards it was the Mods who set the fashion industry on the road to its own 1960s revolution.

The swinging image

In the 1950s, from the time rock 'n' roll hit Britain, the USA ruled teenage trends in the West. Teenagers in the Eastern bloc also fell under the spell. East German adults said that Elvis Presley was America's "secret weapon."

But, in the 1960s, everything changed. In 1963, British teenagers had something new to dance to: *Please Please Me*, the first hit of a quartet of singers from Liverpool. The Beatles had an electrifying effect on their public, first in Britain and then overseas. Suddenly, everything new and exciting seemed to be stamped "Made in Britain." Britain, and especially London, became the world's new capital of teenage style. Mary Quant, whose clothes were already selling in the USA, Europe, Africa, Australia and Canada, was one of its leading ambassadors. But the King's Road now shared its title of London's style headquarters with a narrow and once dingy alleyway in the West End: Carnaby Street.

Carnaby Street and its neighborhood sizzled with life. Teenagers from all over Britain thronged there to buy the latest, trendiest, "gear" or clothes, on sale. Men might go to one of the ten shops owned by John Stephen. Women might buy dresses designed by Sally Tuffin and Marion Foale, two former art students who specialized in a lacy, appealing look. Plenty didn't come to buy at all; they came just to show off what they wore, and see what everyone else was wearing.

Carnaby Street in the 1960s, center of "swinging London," and, together with King's Road, the headquarters of the young fashion scene.

They were being "part of the scene." *Time* magazine, which reported on London style in 1966, coined a name for it all that stuck: "Swinging."

The mass media, printed and electronic, played a crucial part in the youth revolution. They recorded it; they also helped spread it. In Britain, they were going through a revolution of their own at the same time. In 1952, only one person in ten owned a TV. But this total shot up in 1953, after millions had watched coverage of the coronation of Queen Elizabeth. By 1963, TV ownership had spread to 86 per cent of the population.

The year before, an important change had overtaken the British press. Its first-ever color newspaper supplement appeared, a magazine produced by the *Sunday Times*. The cover showed model Jean Shrimpton, wearing a Mary Quant dress in grey flannel. The next year, British radio got a shake-up too, when the "pirate" unregistered radio station Radio Caroline anchored off Felixstowe. Its non-stop broadcasts of pop music were illegal, but an instant hit with the public.

For anyone in the media, the youth revolution had everything that makes a good story: news value, shock value, great sound, great pictures. Television, radio, newspapers and magazines all loved what the youth revolution offered. All of them made money out of the stars of swinging Britain, either by accepting their advertising or just by covering their activities. And the stars made money in return.

Without the media, the fashions of the King's Road and Carnaby Street might have stayed put in London. Even with the media's help, they took time to spread. The mini-skirt, for example, appeared in 1964. It was 1965 before it was seen in what was then the press's headquarters, Fleet Street. By 1967, mini-skirts were still getting shocked glances when British girls wore them in Europe. In the 1970s, they were being worn in other parts of Britain, long after they'd vanished from the London scene. By that time, Britain's swinging image had vanished too. But it left the country with an enduring reputation as a leader of international style.

Mary Quant's reputation and business have endured as well. Today, Mary Quant products range from sunglasses to tights, taking in rainwear, jewelry and mainstream fashion on the way. In 1987, she opened the latest of her international chain of "color shops," selling Quant accessories in Carnaby Street.

Left, in 1965, model Jean Shrimpton wears the new "mini" style on a visit to Australia. "Here's the look," said the British newspaper, the *Daily Mirror*, "that is creating a world demand for British fashions, bringing in millions of pounds in export orders."

Above, fans pack four floors of a London Airport building as the Beatles set off to the Bahamas. The original caption to this photo called them the "most valuable human cargo in show business." They made Britain the pop-music center of the world.

"WITNESS

"These youngsters have become dress conscious largely because they see strikingly dressed young men on TV and in newspapers and magazines. The people who get into the news are well dressed."
Source: Henry Rael-Brook, shirt manufacturer (quoted in *The Fifties*).

"The fashion boom might never have started if the newspapers hadn't backed it up, but now if you go out in Chelsea every single girl looks pretty because she's dressed in the latest clothes, in styles she might never have heard of if she hadn't seen them in some

magazine or newspaper."
Source: *Sunday Times* fashion writer Brigid Keenan (quoted in *The Young Meteors*, Jonathan Aitken, Secker & Warburg, 1967).

"Everyone was against us; the Post Office, the record producers, the Admiralty, the Customs and the Government. In fact, everybody was against us except for the public, who had been waiting for something new in radio for years."
Source: Radio Caroline's first disc-jockey, Simon Dee (quoted in *The Young Meteors*).

Quant in St. Moritz

In the great glittering ballroom, models glided to and fro, swathed in mink stoles. Outside, in the hotel corridor, it was different. They came racing along, only slowing to make their entrance down the grand staircase. On their way, they passed the makeshift dressing station they'd be using later. It was right there in the corridor itself, ready and waiting with the clothes the girls would wear.

It was the only way, Mary Quant thought: the only way to show the clothes fast enough. Through the flu she'd brought with her to St. Moritz, she remembered the day she'd first seen the show rehearsed.

There was that gorgeous ballroom, reached through endless corridors. There were the balldresses that the models would wear most of the time. And there were her own clothes: the fur hats, the knee socks, the boots and red sweaters and short flannel dresses, with their pleats and high waists.

It was no good, trying to show a flannel dress between two ballgowns. It looked all wrong. It didn't look like anything at all. The only way to show the clothes from Bazaar was to show them all together, in a rush. They needed to be seen moving, too: not sailing along like the ballgowns, but dancing, prancing, leaping. That was what her clothes were about. They were about being bouncy, challenging. If that meant challenging the way models usually showed off clothes — well, that was fine.

Suddenly, one of the models came racing up; then another. The others would be here soon. They were off! In a flurry of action, the girls dived into sweaters, pulled up red stockings, hauled flannel tunics over their heads. Outside, jazz rhythms pounded through the ballroom. One after the other, the models shot off and skipped their way down the grand staircase.

The audience gasped, recovered, raved with delight. The women eating and drinking in the ballroom had though they were going to watch an ordinary fashion show. They expected to see clothes like the ones that already hung in their wardrobes. But never, never had the millionaire's ski resort seen clothes like these, shown like this. And one outfit, the last, they would never see again. Backstage, a girl who looked like Greta Garbo scrambled into it, and rushed off to make her entrance at the top of the ballroom stairs.

Above, Mary Quant, who created the "Chelsea Look" and in the 1960s, helped make London the style capital of the world. One of her great achievements was the launch of the mini-skirt, which returned to fashion twenty years later.

Right, over the 1960s and 70s, Mary Quant branched out into specialist design fields such as sportswear, rainwear, hats, and household textiles. For this 1967 photo-call, she used her "crazy" modeling style to show off Quant shoes. Its origins went back to 1957, when she startled the millionaires at the St. Moritz fashion parade.

The audience gasped once more as a Chelsea-style snow princess appeared above them. On her head was a huge white fur hat. She was wrapped in a white fur-trimmed leather coat; white leather boots came up to her knees. The snow princess posed, gripped the edges of her coat, and flung it off. In the rush to get ready, she'd forgotten about putting on . . . a dress.

London already knew about Mary Quant: crazy, zany Mary Quant. After St. Moritz, no one in Europe's world of high fashion would forget her in a hurry.

"The grandees and the millionaires wanted these clothes. They had everything else; all the minks and ball gowns they could use; the silk shirts and the silk trousers; the stretch pants and the leopard tops. But they hadn't any fun clothes. This was something quite new to them and I had no idea to what extent this look was to grip people's imagination and how popular it was to become. Like all women, these pampered people, in spite of their worldly sophistication and possessions, want to look as young as they possibly can and, in a way, this was the beginning of something we take almost for granted now . . . grown-ups wearing teenage fashions and looking like precocious little girls."
Source: Mary Quant, in her autobiography.

"It had begun to dawn on us that by luck . . . by chance . . . perhaps even by mistake . . . we were on to a huge thing. We were in at the beginning of a tremendous renaissance in fashion."
Source: Mary Quant, in her autobiography

"Once only the rich, the Establishment, set the fashion. Now it is the inexpensive little dress seen on the girls in the High (main) Street."
Source: Mary Quant, in her autobiography.

A new design takes shape: Mary Quant at home in the Chelsea apartment that replaced her "bed-sitter factory."

MARY QUANT

In the public eye

Mary Quant was one of the stars of the youth revolution that overtook the world after World War II. She led the group of young British designers who revolutionized the way young women looked. Her great innovation was to make them look younger still. By the mid-1960s, women of all ages aimed to look like "precocious little girls," her own way of putting it.

She also revolutionized the way women thought of fashion. There had been a "little girl" look in the 1920s, too. But it was only in the 1960s that women got used to the idea that clothes could be fun. For many years before that, women had expected their clothes to make them look grander, richer and more sophisticated than they really were. Thanks to the trend Mary Quant started, they found out they could look good in clothes that didn't cost a lot. They could buy them one day, wear them the next, get tired of them soon after, even throw them away. Looking rich was not the point, the main aim was to keep pace with changing style.

A 1960s woman didn't expect her clothes to make her look grander, richer, more sophisticated. Instead, she used them to show what she felt like about herself (or tried to). Quant clothes made women look confident, sparky, full of energy and zip. Their clean even lines and proportions looked good on the over-25s as well as on teenagers.

By pioneering what she called fun clothes, Mary Quant changed huge sections of the fashion industry. She also helped change the way the industry thought about young people who tried to enter it at the top rather than the bottom. When she set up Bazaar, the rest of the trade laughed her off as a "student nut case." Eleven years later the "nut case" went to Buckingham Palace to be honored for her services to fashion.

But her biggest success lay in being a female achiever rather than a young one. The Britain of the "swinging sixties" had almost no time for women executives. In 1968, for example, a survey was carried out of the role women played in running two large British firms. In both, only three managers out of every hundred were female.

Today, 20 years later, there are more women holding senior jobs in Britain. But the numbers are still tiny, and Mary Quant is still one of the few British women in industry who have made it to the top.

Honored for services to fashion: Mary Quant, wearing the mini-skirt she launched, receives an award at Buckingham Palace in 1966.

BIOGRAPHY

1934 Born Mary Quant, in London.
1949–1952 Studies art at Goldsmiths' College, where she meets Alexander Plunket Greene.
1955 With Alexander and photographer Archie McNair, opens the boutique Bazaar in Chelsea's King's Road; starts designing clothes for it.
1957 At a fashion show at St. Moritz, invents her fast-paced technique of showing clothes. Marries Alexander; later has one child. Opens second boutique in Knightsbridge; scores big hit with British fashion press.
1962 First visit to USA ends in major success with US fashion press; is signed up by US chain store to design for them; enters mass production.
1963 Wins *Sunday Times* "Woman of the Year" award. Launches Mary Quant's Ginger Group to manufacture dresses and sportswear for international market.
1966 "Youthquake" tour of US; branches into cosmetics. Receives the honor, the "Order of the British Empire" for services to fashion.
1970 Branches into household furnishings and textiles.
1973 London Museum exhibits her work.
1982 Branches into shoes and children's wear.
1987 Opens new shop, in Carnaby Street.

"Her revolution soon became an institution and the trickle of 'mods' welled up into a torrent of swingers. Boutiques proliferated, designers multiplied, journalists, models and photographers leapt gleefully on to the rolling band-wagon, giving the cult massive impetus by massive publicity. Soon a vast new industry was born, today employing an estimated 30,000 people all dedicated to selling clothes to the young and the young at heart."
Source: Jonathan Aitken, writing in *The Young Meteors*.

"Today's fashion could not have developed without the revolution of the Sixties; and our boutiques, bistros, coffee bars and discotheques are all a heritage of that decade. . . . Mary Quant, John Bates, Ossie Clarke and many other Sixties designers continue to influence the fashion of today."
Source: Barbara Bernard, in *Fashion in the 60's*, Academy Editions, 1978. ❞❞

Quant designs, marked with their distinctive "daisy," have brought business and jobs to industries that range from umbrella-making to cosmetics. Here, photographed in 1970, Mary Quant is watching how Quant mascara is processed.

Conclusion

Women have always taken part in industry. Before the Industrial Revolution made mass production possible, they based their industries at home, just as Third World women do today. Most families then had to be self-sufficient. Women shared with men the work of providing things to eat, to wear, and to make day-to-day life more convenient. If they could, they also made goods at home they could sell: things like yarn for weaving into textiles.

If they were rich, like Catharine Greene, they would not make goods themselves. But they would share the work of managing the way their households and family businesses or industries were run. If their husbands were away, they might have to make all the main decisions themselves. This could also happen if they were widowed, like Nicole-Barbe Clicquot. Many women would have backed away from the task she took on. Very few people, women or men, could have run her family business as well as she did. But, at that time, there was nothing unusual about her decision.

Over a hundred years divide these two women from Mary Quant. Very few women made industrial history in the middle and late nineteenth centuries. The reason is that the Industrial Revolution took industry out of the home and into factories. Many women worked in these factories. But it became much more difficult for them to have any say in how the work was done.

The factories made money for the men who owned them and made the decisions. But now their wives could not share their work and responsibilities. They were still tied to their homes by pregnancies and childcare duties, just as they always had been. People soon started to feel that women and industrial decisions didn't go together. It was not "ladylike" or "feminine" to run an industrial-based business.

This attitude has modified during the present century. But it has not disappeared. As the time chart shows, women have made most impact in industries that used to be home-based anyway: fashion, catering, make-up. And, even today, women company directors like Mary Quant are extremely scarce. In Britain, for example, they are outnumbered thirty to one by men. Today's women in industry do not have to fight against invading armies as in the days of Veuve Clicquot. But prejudice, lack of opportunity, and low expectations from women themselves have effects that are just as crippling.

BOOKS TO READ

USA
Essential reading:
Caty: a Biography of Catharine Littlefield Greene, by John F. Stegeman and Janet A. Stegeman; first published by the Rhode Island Bicentennial Foundation, 1977; re-printed by the University of Georgia Press, 1985.

Very useful: **The world of Eli Whitney**, Jeannette Mirsky and Allan Nevins, Macmillan (NY) 1952; and **Eli Whitney and the Birth of American Technology**, Constance M. Green, Little, Brown (Boston and Toronto), 1956. The standard works on Whitney, written for adults, but highly readable. Ask your local library to get them.

Founding Mothers: Women of America in the Revolutionary Era by Linda G. DePauw, Houghton, Mifflin (Boston), 1975.

FRANCE
Essential reading:
Champagne: the Wine, the Land and the People, by Patrick Forbes, David & Charles (North Pomfret, VT), 1967.

This is *the* book on champagne; get it through your library. Don't be discouraged by its length; use the index to track down references to Veuve Clicquot.

Very useful: **A Wine Tour of France** by Frederick S. Wildman, Jr., Random House (New York), 1976. Like all books on wine, this is written for adults. But it has an excellent chapter on Veuve Clicquot, and good pictures.

Living Through History: The French Revolution by Robert and Elizabeth Campling, David & Charles (North Pomfret, VT), 1984.

GREAT BRITAIN
Essential reading; Mary Quant's autobiography, **Quant by Quant**, G. P. Putnam's Sons (NY), 1966. Available in public libraries only.

Also read **Color by Quant: Your Complete Personal Guide to Beauty and Fashion** by Mary Quant, McGraw-Hill and Co. (New York), 1985.

Also useful: **Costumes and Clothes** by Jean Cooke, The Bookwright Press (New York), 1987.

Women in Business by Laura French and Diana Stewart, Raintree Publishers (Milwaukee, WI), 1979.

Her first job interview. In 1961, when this picture was taken, this young woman was in her teens. By now, she will be in her mid-40s. At this age, if she were a man, she would be at the peak of her career.

But few of the top people in business and industry are women. One reason for this is public attitudes, but another reason is very practical. If a woman has a baby, she has to stop work for a while. If she wants to go back to work, she has to find someone else to take care of it during the day. Childcare can be difficult to arrange and expensive.

She may decide to take part-time work instead. Or she may decide to stay at home until her children are at school, and then go back to work. When she does, she may find that making up for those "lost" years is very difficult.

People are now more aware of the special problems women face in their working lives, but there is still an enormous amount to be done before women's chances of reaching the top are really equal to men's.

Time chart

1792: USA
Catharine Greene, widow of a Georgia plantation owner, inspires and later finances the invention of the cotton gin.

1794: France
Marie Grosholtz inherits from her uncle the collection of wax portraits they have made. Later takes her waxworks exhibition to Britain, where she sets it up under her married name: **Madame Tussaud.**

1805: France
Newly-widowed **Nicole-Barbe Clicquot** decides to run her dead husband's champagne business.

1857: Britain
Emily Faithfull fights male domination of the printing trade by setting up an all-woman printing firm in Edinburgh.

1858: France
Louise Pommery, wife of the head of the Pommery champagne firm, is widowed; follows Madame Clicquot's example by taking over her husband's business.

1901: USA
Sarah Breedlove Walker, a black woman from the Deep South, invents a range of hair straighteners and other beauty products for black women; later becomes a millionaire.

1908: Britain
Polish-born **Helena Rubinstein** opens the first European branch of her cosmetics business is London; later to be followed by branches in Paris and the USA.

1912: USA
Canadian-born Florence Graham launches her cosmetics company, named **"Elizabeth Arden,"** in New York.

1939: USA
Dorothy Schiff becomes proprietor of the *New York Post*, which she manages until 1976.

1954: France
Dress designer **Gabrielle Chanel** comes out of retirement to launch the still-acclaimed Chanel "look."

1955: Britain
Mary Quant launches Bazaar and starts designing clothes for it.

Glossary

American Civil War
1861–1865. The war between the Northern and Southern states.

American War of Independence
1776–1781. America fought the "Revolutionary War" to free itself from British colonial rule.

Arkwright's Water Frame One of the technological breakthroughs that powered the British Industrial Revolution (see below). Invented in 1769, it was a large water-powered machine for spinning thread. Because it was big, it had to be housed in a special workplace; a "manufactory," or factory.

Bed-sitter A tiny studio apartment where the bedroom and "sitting" room are the same.

Boutique Shop specializing in stylish clothes, usually for young buyers.

Champagne Sparkling (fizzy) white wine produced in the Champagne district of France.

Cambric Fine linen material; lawn is the same.

Chelsea Riverside district in central London; formerly a cheap area loved by artists and writers. When Mary Quant worked there, it was about to lose its "arty" image. It is now very expensive.

"Chelsea Look" The spirited younger-looking fashion of dressing created by Mary Quant and others in the 1950s; colored stockings and high boots were important features.

Cotton gin The machine invented by Eli Whitney, with Catharine Greene's help, to clean seeds from American green-seed (or upland) cotton. Later versions were called "saw-gins."

"Cotton Kingdom" The area of the USA where upland cotton was (and still is) grown; covering most, but not all, of the South-Eastern states.

Crompton's Mule A spinning machine invented in 1776. It was the combination of the mule with water power, first used in 1790, which most effectively shifted the process of spinning into factories.

French Revolution The revolt of the French people against their despotic rulers, which began in 1789. From the turmoil which followed, Napoleon Bonaparte emerged as France's supreme leader.

Guillotine Instrument of execution that cuts off the victim's head. Notorious for its use in the French Revolution.

Hargreaves' Spinning Jenny Invented around 1767, this was one of the earliest automatic spinning machines. It was small enough to be used at home.

Harrods One of London's most famous (and expensive) department stores.

Industrial Revolution The major change, started in Britain, that took place in systems of production in the late 18th and early 19th centuries. Muscle power was replaced by steam or water power. The use of machines meant a change in place of work from home to factory.

King's Road One of the best-known streets in Chelsea; famous for its shops and the style of the people who shop there.

"Klikoskoe" The Russian version of Madame Clicquot's name; the name given in Russia to her champagne.

Plantation Originally, a privately-owned unit of land in colonial America; later, a large farm in the Southern states of the US. Plantation work was done by black slaves. The owners were called planters.

Pupitre The French for "desk." In champagne-making a *pupitre* is the sloping rack on which bottles undergo the *remuage* process.

Remuage Process used in champagne manufacture for making the sediment (see below) in a bottle slide down on top of the cork, after which it can easily be removed. Invented by Nicole-Barbe Clicquot.

Sediment Small particles of solid matter present in wine.

Skiffle Folk-based, do-it-yourself form of teenage music, very popular in Britain in the 1950s.

"Swinging London" The name coined, originally by *Time* magazine, to describe Britain's status as the leader of youth culture in the mid-1960s. The Sixties themselves were also called "Swinging."

Union The union of states forming the United States of America. The Civil War started because the Southern states left, or seceded from, the Union.

Index

PLACES TO VISIT

Visiting the following places may help you understand more about the people and industries in this book. Some of the organizations can give you extra information. Write to them to ask what services they can offer, and whether it's possible to make an appointment to visit them.

FRANCE
Veuve Clicquot Ponsardin, 12 Rue du Temple, 51100 Reims, France. (The firm organizes visits to its cellars at 1 Place des Droits de l'Homme, Reims.)

GREAT BRITAIN
The Champagne Bureau, 14 Pall Mall, London SW1 5LU.
Carnaby Street Now a pedestrian zone running parallel to Regent Street in London. Look out for Mary Quant's newly-opened Colour Shop.
King's Road, Chelsea, London. Mary Quant's Bazaar, at Number 138A, is no longer there. But King's Road itself is still famous for its style.

USA
The Georgia Local History Society, 501 Whitaker Street, Savannah, Georgia 31499, USA. Savannah was the nearest town to Mulberry Grove, 12 miles distant. But Catharine Greene's house no longer exists.